LOOK AROUND

SHOPS

Clive Pace and Jean Birch

How to use this book

Use this book to help you discover things about the shops in your town. Try to find out as much as you can. The answers to some of the questions are at the back of the book, but don't look at them until you have tried to work them out for yourself. Some of the questions only you can answer because they are about the town you live in.

Never go to the shops without first asking your parents' permission. When you are out, always remember to be very careful. Stay on the pavement and never cross the road without help from an adult. Never talk to strangers.

Look Around You

Look Around Homes
Look Around the Park
Look Around the School
Look Around Shops
Look Around the Street
Look Around Transport

Editor: Alison Cooper
Designer: Ross George

First published in 1989 by
Wayland (Publishers) Ltd
61 Western Road, Hove
East Sussex BN3 1JD, England

British Library Cataloguing in Publication Data
Pace, Clive L.
  Shops
  1. Shops – For Children
  I. Title II. Birch, Jean.   III. Series
  381'.1

HARDBACK ISBN 1 85210 471 6

PAPERBACK ISBN 0 7502 0556 3

Phototypeset by Kalligraphic Design Ltd, Horley, Surrey
Printed and bound in Belgium by Casterman S.A.

Contents

Answers to questions are on page 28.
The words that are <u>underlined</u>
appear in the glossary on page 29.

THE LOCAL SHOP

What does your nearest shop sell?

It might be a corner shop on its own.
Or it might be in a <u>parade.</u>

You can usually buy a lot of different things in corner shops. They often sell anything from newspapers to milk, from shoelaces to shampoo. Sometimes there is a post office counter.

Have you noticed how late most corner shops often stay open?
Why is this?

What do you think this shop sells?

8

Look at a parade of shops if there is one near where you live.

What does each shop sell?
Do they all sell different things?

In a parade of shops you might find a butcher, a baker and a chemist.

What other shops might be useful in a parade?

LARGE SHOPS

The shop you visit most is probably the supermarket. Some of these are very large.

How often do you go to the supermarket?

How is it different from other shops?

People often travel by car to the supermarket. They can buy their whole week's groceries in one go.

What else can you buy in your supermarket?

10

Superstores are another kind of big shop. They are often on the edge of a town where there is plenty of room for a very large shop and lots of space to park cars.

What does this superstore sell?
▼   ▼

Do you know what other superstores sell?

If your parents have bought a lot of <u>bulky</u> items, they may be able to hire a roof-rack for their car, or a van ▶ like this to carry them home.

INTERNATIONAL SHOPS

International shops sell goods from different countries. You might find shops selling Indian or Pakistani goods, a Polish <u>delicatessen</u> or a Chinese supermarket.

These shops used to serve their own <u>communities.</u> Nowadays lots of people go there specially to shop for the unusual foods they sell.

Try to find out what countries are represented in shops around your home.

◀ Do you know what this man is selling?

Have you ever tried any of them?

What countries do they come from?

This shop sells clothing sometimes worn by Asian women.
▼

MOBILE SHOPS

Mobile shops are usually vans which come to your street.

They go to areas where people find it difficult to get to ordinary shops. They often visit housing estates on the edge of towns.

The shopkeeper usually comes at the same time and on the same day each week.

Can you think why?

When the mobile shop arrives, the driver usually rings a bell or sounds the horn. This tells everyone that the shop is open.

Some mobile shops sell groceries. Others sell fresh fish or vegetables.

Most old people find mobile shops very convenient.

Do you know why?

◄ The ice-cream van might be your favourite mobile shop.

Do any other mobile shops visit your street?

SHOPS FOR TRAVELLERS

Petrol stations are a different kind of shop. They mainly sell petrol, but many now sell lots of other things as well.

Drivers can buy things that they need for their cars, such as oil, tools and car polish. They can also often buy sweets, crisps, drinks and other snacks for long journeys.

Sometimes you can buy the most unexpected things. When you next go to a petrol station, find out what else you can buy.

Railway and bus stations also have shops for travellers.

Here you will also find snacks and drinks for the journey. Usually there are lots of newspapers, magazines, comics and books for sale too.

People often like to read while travelling by bus or train.

What other kinds of shops have you seen at a railway station?

What do you like to do on a long journey?

A travel agency is another kind of shop for travellers.

What does a travel agency sell?

MARKETS

Have you ever been to a market?

Many towns have a market day. The stall-holders travel to the town and set up their stalls in the market place. They move from town to town on different days.

▲

They arrive early to set out their goods on the stalls.

◀ Many stalls have colourful awnings. These protect the stalls from the rain.

Is there a market day in your town?

Is there an indoor market as well?

You can buy almost anything in a market.

There are stalls that sell fruit and vegetables, pots and pans, clothes, fabrics and toys.

Can you think of any others?

The market is often a noisy place. The stall-holders shout to attract customers to come and buy from their stall.

Why do you think markets are such busy places?

TAKE-AWAY FOOD SHOPS

◀ The most common take-away food shop is the fish and chip shop.

As well as fish and chips, these shops sell other kinds of hot food.

What does your local fish and chip shop sell?

There are many other kinds of take-away food shops.

The people who own them may come from all over the world and they often sell food from their home countries.

What kinds of take-away food shops are there near where you live?
Do any of them sell food from other countries?

You may find a Chinese or Indian take-away. ▶

◀ Or a Turkish <u>doner kebab</u> house.

◀ Or an Italian pizzeria.

Have you tried any of these foods? Which do you like best?

CHARITY SHOPS

Do you know what a charity shop is?
How is it different from other shops?

▲

Some well-known charity shops are run by organizations such as Oxfam, Save the Children, and Barnardo's.

Do you know what work these charities do?

Most of the things sold in charity shops have been given by people who no longer need them. Some things are new.

Other goods are sold to advertise the charity. They often have the charity's sign or <u>logo</u> on them.

◄ This is the logo for Help the Aged.

Some shops support local charities. They try to help people by raising money for local groups and hospitals.

Try to find out about the work of a local charity shop.

SHOPPING CENTRES

Many towns have a new shopping centre where the shops are all under cover.

These centres are often on ▶ different levels which are connected by lifts and <u>escalators</u>.

Sometimes there are eating ▶ areas which are like pavement cafés. You can choose from many different <u>kiosks</u>. Often there are plants, trees and running water which make the eating area look as if it is outside.

The shops are on <u>pedestrian walkways</u>. Some of the shops do not have doors. The fronts of the shops are open.

▼

Do you know why?

Many of the well-known <u>chain stores</u> have a shop in these centres. You will often find a large chemist's shop, and stores selling electrical goods, shoes, clothes, records and <u>stationery</u>.

►

Have you seen any of these shops in your town?

Why do you think people like shopping in indoor shopping centres?

PAVEMENT DISPLAYS

Many shops attract customers by making a <u>display</u> outside the shop. These displays show some of the things they have for sale.

▼

It is easy for people to see the goods and choose what they want to buy.

You will often find fruit, vegetables and flowers displayed in this way, but sometimes you will see other things which are more unusual.

This is a display of fridges. ►

What unusual things have you seen displayed outside a shop?

Shopkeepers who cannot display their goods outside often put an eye-catching sign on the pavement.

What kind of shops do you think these signs are advertising?

▼ ▼ ▼

What different signs can you find on the pavement?

The next time you go shopping, look out for the interesting things you have read about in this book.

What did you find out?

Page 8:
Corner shops stay open late so that they can sell things that people need when other shops are closed.
This is a chemist's shop. It sells medicines, soap, shampoos, make-up, and many other items which you might find in your bathroom or first-aid box.

Page 10:
A **supermarket** is a shop in which the customers serve themselves. Supermarkets often sell many different goods, but ordinary shops usually sell only one type, such as clothes, shoes or bread.

Page 11:
This **superstore** sells do-it-yourself goods and all kinds of gardening items.

Page 13:
On the stall there are yams and water melons that grow in Africa, sweet potatoes from South America and green bananas from the West Indies.

Page 14:
Mobile shopkeepers usually come on the same day each week so that people will know when to expect them.

Page 15:
Old people do not have to go very far to shop. The **mobile shop** comes to them.

Page 17:
You may have seen flower shops, gift shops, chemists, and <u>kiosks</u> where people can hire a car.
A **travel agency** sells airline and ferry tickets and arranges holidays.

Page 19:
Other stalls often sell shoes, flowers, books, china, eggs and cheese, second-hand goods and many other things.
Lots of people go to **markets** because the goods are usually cheaper than in the shops.

Page 22:
The money that a **charity shop** makes goes to help run the charity. Most of the people who work in charity shops are not paid. In other shops, the money goes to the owners. They pay the people who work there.

Page 25:
The open front makes it much easier for people to walk into the shop. They can also see what is inside the shop.
People like shopping in indoor **shopping centres** because they are protected from bad weather and they do not have to worry about avoiding traffic.

Page 27:
The sign on the left is advertising a butcher's shop. The sign on the right shows it is a newsagent's.

Glossary

Bulky   Very large and difficult to carry.

Chain stores   A series of shops owned by the same firm. They can be found in most large towns.

Communities   Groups of people who live in the same area.

Delicatessen   A shop that sells food that has already been cooked or prepared, especially different kinds of cooked meats.

Display   The way shopkeepers arrange their goods. This is so that customers and people passing by can see what the shop has for sale.

Doner kebab   Small pieces of grilled meat and vegetables held together on a long wooden or metal pin called a skewer.

Escalators   Moving staircases for carrying people up or down.

Kiosks   Very small shops with open fronts. Customers do not usually go inside but are served across a counter.

Logo   A special symbol or sign.

Parade   A row of shops.

Pedestrian walkways   Wide areas between shops which people walk along. There is no traffic and the walkways are often on different levels.

Stationery   Writing paper, envelopes, pens, pencils and all other articles needed for writing and typing.

Further reading

Behind the scenes: Supermarkets by Andrew Langley (Franklin Watts, 1983)
Behind the scenes: McDonald's by Susan Pepper (Franklin Watts, 1985)
Markets by Sarah Allen (CUP, 1983)
Supermarkets by Tim Wood (Franklin Watts, 1988)

Index

Picture Acknowledgements

J. Allan Cash 15, 18 (bottom), 21 (top right), 22, 23 (top), 24 (top), 26 (top); Jean Birch 19; Bruce Coleman 14; C. L. Pace 9, 10, 11 (top left, bottom), 12, 13 (bottom), 16, 21 (bottom), 25, 26 (bottom), 27; Topham Picture Library 13 (top); Wayland Picture Library (Richard Sharpley & Julia Waterlow) 8, 11 (top right), 17 (bottom), 18 (top), 20, 21 (top left), 24 (bottom); Tim Woodcock cover; Zefa 17 (top). The illustration on page 23 is by Malcolm Walker.